242
.14
Pra

D0387915

Thank
God

Thank God

STORIES *of* GRATITUDE, HARVEST, *and* HOME

PARACLETE PRESS
BREWSTER, MASSACHUSETTS

Thank God: Stories of Gratitude, Harvest, and Home

2011 First printing

Copyright © 2011 by Paraclete Press

ISBN 978-1-55725-979-0

Scriptural references are taken from the New Revised Standard Version Bible, copyright © 1989 by the Division of Education of the National Council of Churches of Christ in the U.S.A., and are used by permission. All rights reserved.

The quotations from Sister Bridget Haase are taken from *Generous Faith* (Brewster, MA: Paraclete Press, 2009) and are used by permission.

Library of Congress Cataloging-in-Publication Data

Thank God: stories of gratitude, harvest, and home / by Paraclete Press.
    p. cm.
  ISBN 978-1-55725-979-0 (hard cover)
 1. Gratitude—Religious aspects—Christianity. 2. Christian life. I. Paraclete Press.
  BV4647.G8T435 2011
  241′.4—dc23

                                                    2011022631

10 9 8 7 6 5 4 3 2 1

All rights reserved. No portion of this book may be reproduced, stored in an electronic retrieval system, or transmitted in any form or by any means—electronic, mechanical, photocopy, recording, or any other—except for brief quotations in printed reviews, without the prior permission of the publisher.

Published by Paraclete Press
Brewster, Massachusetts
www.paracletepress.com

Printed in the United States of America

Contents

Introduction

There is an old proverb from Eastern Europe that says, "Who does not thank for little, will not thank for much."

In other words, the person who goes through life being thankful for God's gifts and blessings usually experiences more of life's goodness—and inhabits more of God's blessings.

With this book, we challenge you to live in a way that blesses God from whom all good things come. If you will do this, and become a person of gratitude, giving thanks for all of the good things in your life—even those things that are painful, or beyond understanding—you may expect to see your life transformed before your eyes.

The Doxology
Praise God from whom all blessings flow,
Praise Him all creatures here below.
Praise Him above ye heavenly hosts,
Praise Father, Son, and Holy Ghost.
Amen.

Praise and faith strengthen and nourish one another. That is why St. Paul says, "Do not worry about anything, but in everything by prayer and supplication *with thanksgiving* let your requests be made known to God" (Philippians 4:6).

Gratitude binds our hearts to God and to each other, destroying the walls that divide us. Gratitude is the key that unlocks the inner treasury of grace.

Gratitude is an antidote to false pride, and the remedy for fear. Gratitude opens the channels of fellowship and charity, because it kills false competition and jealousy. Showing gratitude to God by praising him actually opens clogged channels, so that our souls can grow stronger in the pure sunlight of God's love and goodness.

It is a simple fact of life and faith. As you practice gratitude, you will be flooded with more and more good things. And you will become aware of the beauty and goodness that were there in your life all along. Your eyes will open to the world in a new way.

And you will become a blessing to those around you as never before. As Robert Louis Stevenson said, "Every heart that has beat strongly and cheerfully has left a hopeful impulse behind it in the world, and bettered the tradition of mankind."

A Prayer of Thanksgiving

(for any occasion)

For each new morning with its light,

For rest and shelter of the night,

For health and food,

For love and friends,

For everything Thy goodness sends.

—RALPH WALDO EMERSON
(1803–1882)

Beauty All Around Us

Poems and Praise

Sonnet 73

WILLIAM SHAKESPEARE

That time of year thou mayst in me behold
When yellow leaves, or none, or few, do hang
Upon those boughs which shake against the cold,
Bare ruined choirs, where late the sweet birds sang.
In me thou see'st the twilight of such day
As after sunset fadeth in the west;
Which by and by black night doth take away,
Death's second self, that seals up all in rest.
In me thou see'st the glowing of such fire,
That on the ashes of his youth doth lie,
As the deathbed whereon it must expire,
Consumed with that which it was nourished by.
This thou perceiv'st, which makes thy love more strong,
To love that well which thou must leave ere long.

(1609)

God has two dwellings; one in heaven,
and the other in a meek and thankful heart.
—IZAAK WALTON

To Autumn

WILLIAM BLAKE

O Autumn, laden with fruit, and stain'd
With the blood of the grape, pass not, but sit
Beneath my shady roof; there thou may'st rest,
And tune thy jolly voice to my fresh pipe,
And all the daughters of the year shall dance!
Sing now the lusty song of fruits and flowers.

"The narrow bud opens her beauties to
The sun, and love runs in her thrilling veins;
Blossoms hang round the brows of Morning, and
Flourish down the bright cheek of modest Eve,
Till clust'ring Summer breaks forth into singing,
And feather'd clouds strew flowers round her head.

"The spirits of the air live in the smells
Of fruit; and Joy, with pinions light, roves round
The gardens, or sits singing in the trees."
Thus sang the jolly Autumn as he sat,
Then rose, girded himself, and o'er the bleak
Hills fled from our sight; but left his golden load.

(1783)

A thankful heart is not only the greatest virtue,
but the parent of all other virtues.

—CICERO

Autumn Fires

ROBERT LOUIS STEVENSON

In the other gardens
  And all up the vale,
From the autumn bonfires
  See the smoke trail!

Pleasant summer over
  And all the summer flowers,
The red fire blazes,
  The gray smoke towers.

Sing a song of seasons!
  Something bright in all!
Flowers in the summer,
  Fires in the fall!

(1913)

Autumn in the Garden

HENRY VAN DYKE

When the frosty kiss of Autumn in the dark
Makes its mark
On the flowers, and the misty morning grieves
Over fallen leaves;
Then my olden garden, where the golden soil
Through the toil
Of a hundred years is mellow, rich, and deep,
Whispers in its sleep.

'Mid the crumpled beds of marigold and phlox,
Where the box
Borders with its glossy green the ancient walks,
There's a voice that talks
Of the human hopes that bloomed and withered here
Year by year,—
Dreams of joy, that brightened all the labouring hours,
Fading as the flowers.

Yet the whispered story does not deepen grief;
But relief
For the loneliness of sorrow seems to flow
From the Long-Ago,

When I think of other lives that learned, like mine,
To resign,
And remember that the sadness of the fall
Comes alike to all.

What regrets, what longings for the lost were theirs!
And what prayers
For the silent strength that nerves us to endure
Things we cannot cure!
Pacing up and down the garden where they paced,
I have traced
All their well-worn paths of patience, till I find
Comfort in my mind.

Faint and far away their ancient griefs appear:
Yet how near
Is the tender voice, the careworn, kindly face,
Of the human race!
Let us walk together in the garden, dearest heart,
Not apart!
They who know the sorrows other lives have known
Never walk alone.

(1903)

There are only two ways to live your life.
One is as though nothing is a miracle.
The other is as though everything is a miracle.
—ALBERT EINSTEIN

Psalm 107:1

Give thanks to the Lord, for he is good;
for his steadfast love endures for ever.

Keep a green tree in your heart and perhaps
a singing bird will come.
—CHINESE PROVERB

Be glad of life because it gives you the chance to love
and to work and to play and to look at the stars.
—HENRY VAN DYKE

Almighty God, Father of all mercies, we your unworthy servants give you most humble and hearty thanks for all your goodness and loving-kindness to us and to all people. We bless you for our creation, preservation, and all the blessings of this life; but above all for your inestimable love in the redemption of the world by our Lord Jesus Christ, for the means of grace, and for the hope of glory. And we ask you, give us a true understanding of all your mercies, so that our hearts may be unreservedly thankful, and so that we show forth your praise not only with our lips but in our lives; by giving up ourselves to your service, and by walking before you in holiness and righteousness all our days. We ask this through Jesus Christ our Lord, to whom with you and the Holy Ghost be all honor and glory, world without end. Amen.

—Traditional prayer of "General Thanksgiving"

15

Our National Thanksgiving
SARAH JOSEPHA HALE

This following was written by Sarah Josepha Hale, known as "The Mother of American Thanksgiving" for the way in which she campaigned to have the day recognized throughout the United States. She would convince President Abraham Lincoln to proclaim an annual National Day of Thanksgiving in 1863.

All the blessings of the fields,
All the stores the garden yields,
All the plenty summer pours,
Autumn's rich, o'erflowing stores,
Peace, prosperity and health,
Private bliss and public wealth,
Knowledge with its gladdening streams,
Pure religion's holier beams—
Lord, for these our souls shall raise
Grateful vows and solemn praise.

We are most happy to agree with the large majority of the governors of the different States—as shown in their unanimity of action for several past years, and which, we hope, will this year be adopted by all—that the last Thursday in November shall be the DAY of NATIONAL THANKSGIVING for the American people. Let this day, from this time forth, as long as our Banner of Stars floats on the breeze, be the grand THANKSGIVING HOLIDAY of our nation, when the noise and tumult of worldliness may be exchanged for the laugh of happy children, the glad greetings of family reunion, and the humble gratitude of the Christian heart. This truly American Festival falls, this year on the twenty-fifth day of this month.

Let us consecrate the day to benevolence of action, by sending good gifts to the poor, and doing those deeds of charity that will, for one day, make every American home the place of plenty and of rejoicing. These seasons of refreshing are of inestimable advantage to the popular heart; and, if rightly managed, will greatly aid and strengthen public harmony of feeling. Let the people of all the States and Territories sit down together to the "feast of fat things," and drink, in the sweet draught of joy and gratitude to the Divine giver of all our blessings, the pledge of renewed love to the Union, and to each other; and of peace and good-will to all men. Then the last Thursday in November will soon become the day of AMERICAN THANKSGIVING throughout the world.

—From the "Editor's Table," *Godey's Lady's Book,* 1858

Thanksgiving Day Proclamation

ABRAHAM LINCOLN

This proclamation was delivered to the American people on October 3, 1863. To this day, each American president delivers a new Thanksgiving Day proclamation each year, honoring what was started by the sixteenth president.

The year that is drawing towards its close, has been filled with the blessings of fruitful fields and healthful skies. To these bounties, which are so constantly enjoyed that we are prone to forget the source from which they come, others have been added, which are of so extraordinary a nature, that they cannot fail to penetrate and soften even the heart which is habitually insensible to the ever watchful providence of Almighty God. In the midst of a civil war of unequalled magnitude and severity, which has sometimes seemed to foreign States to invite and to provoke their aggression, peace has been preserved with all nations, order has been maintained, the laws have been respected and obeyed, and harmony has prevailed everywhere except in the theatre of military conflict; while that theatre has been greatly contracted by the advancing armies and navies of the Union. Needful diversions of wealth and of strength from the fields of peaceful industry to the national defence, have not arrested the plough, the shuttle, or the ship; the axe had enlarged the borders of our settlements, and the mines, as well of iron and coal as of the precious metals, have yielded even more abundantly than heretofore. Population has steadily increased, notwithstanding the waste that has been made in the camp, the siege and the battle-field; and the country, rejoicing in the consciousness of augmented strength and vigor, is permitted to expect continuance of years with large increase of freedom. No human counsel hath devised nor hath any mortal hand worked out these great things. They are the gracious gifts of the Most High God, who, while dealing with us in anger for our sins, hath nevertheless remembered mercy. It has seemed to me fit and proper that they should be solemnly, reverently and gratefully acknowledged as with one heart and voice by the whole American People. I do therefore invite my fellow citizens in every part of the United States, and also those who are at sea and those who are sojourning in foreign lands, to set apart and observe the last Thursday of November next, as a day of Thanksgiving and Praise to our beneficent Father who dwelleth in the Heavens. And I recommend to them that while offering up the ascriptions justly due to Him for such singular deliverances and blessings, they do also, with humble penitence for our national perverseness and disobedience, commend to his tender care all those who have become widows, orphans, mourners or sufferers in the lamentable civil strife in which we are unavoidably engaged, and fervently implore the interposition of the Almighty Hand to heal the wounds of the nation and to restore it as soon as may be consistent with the Divine purposes to the full enjoyment of peace, harmony, tranquillity and Union. It is the duty of nations as well as of men to own their dependence upon the overruling power of God; to confess their sins and transgressions in humble sorrow, yet with assured hope that genuine repentance will lead to mercy and pardon; and to recognize the sublime truth, announced in the Holy Scriptures and proven by all history, that those nations are blessed whose God is the Lord.

Give thanks in all circumstances; for this is the
will of God in Christ Jesus for you.
—1 THESSALONIANS 5:18

25

Three Reflections
on an Attitude of Sharing

SISTER BRIDGET HAASE

A Church Lady's Holiday

How do I feel when those in need
want to ease my life's burdens?

It was a Thanksgiving etched in memory.

For several months, I had been living in Sandy Lick Hollow in the hills of West Virginia, sharing life and lessons of the heart with my mountain-folk neighbors.

Delena and Elam lived two miles deep in a hollow. The dirt road, muddy, rugged, and often strewn with fallen branches, made my trip there both a challenge and a risk. I often wondered how they were ever able to get out, never mind how often.

"Home" was a ramshackle dwelling, hardly worthy to be called a "house." It was there that Delena and Elam raised their five children and a host of stray animals in need of shelter.

Their destitution was accentuated by cruel judgments and a mountain prejudice. They were shunned by neighbors who deemed them unfit and callously referred to them as "poor white trash."

Early one evening in late October, Delena and Elam came to visit for the first time. They had chugged their hour trip in a borrowed truck, long overdue for a safety check. They climbed the stairs to the porch, one hesitant step at a time. I sensed their concern. I was certain that they had come for material assistance, and I began to mentally calculate how many potatoes, cans of beans, how much milk, wood, or coal I could reasonably spare.

Suddenly Elam's words broke my thoughts.

"We'd be rightly honored if you would join us for Thanksgiving dinner. You're a long way from home, and it's a family day. We're asking early 'cuz we'd like to plan."

Filled with uncertainty, doubt, and longing, Delena's eyes caught mine.

"I am delighted with your gracious invitation," I replied. "I'll be there."

"Bring nothing. Nothing at all," called Elam as they got back into the truck.

Thanksgiving Day arrived. It was cold but snow-free as I began the trek to the hollow and to a holiday dinner with friends.

Pity for their situation overwhelmed me as I entered their home. There was no water, no electricity, no indoor plumbing. Flattened cardboard boxes taped together formed the walls that encircled the family and kept the winter cold at bay. The coal stove, intended to heat all the rooms, actually heated only one.

The children squealed with delight when I arrived. They ushered me in to "sit for a spell" to warm up and to catch up, so I took my place close to the coal stove. Delena said it was good to feel the warmth of life and blessings on such a day as this.

"Come to the table," Elam invited.

We all gathered around, held hands, and offered prayers of thanksgiving for all we had been given—our ongoing friendship, enough food, the children, the creek and abundant well water, summer pole beans and sun-ripened tomatoes, purple irises on the hills and blue chicory along the roadsides, the wood for the stove—and all that was yet to come. Then we took our places.

As I looked at my place, I could see that Delena had neatly arranged the best plate in the house, a Mason jar glass, a spoon, and a fork. She, Elam and the children shared the remaining two plates, three forks, and two Mason jars.

My eye caught the decorations for such a festive occasion. Some sprigs from a pine tree spruced up an old jar. The cardboard walls facing me were decorated with pine cones and fir branches and held a boldly written message: "A big welcome to the church lady."

As soon as Elam offered me a plate with some sort of meat covered in oil, I sensed a challenge.

"Good, strong, wild meat," he said. "Been savin' it for just such a time."

I helped myself to the unidentified dish, knowing it couldn't stay on the plate and hoping it would stay down. I thought it best not to ask what made the meat strong and wild.

Then Delena offered me "the last greens picked before the frost got 'em all, and the mushrooms are from the summer. They been stored real good and should be fine."

I am sure she did not say "should be fine" in the emphatic way it sounded.

The meal went on. Eating, laughing, singing together a spirit-filled rendition of "The Old Rugged Cross" made thoughts of turkey, cranberry, and pumpkin pie oozing with whipped cream disappear into the cold air, and the reality of mystery meat and stale mushrooms find a resting place.

Before long, darkness began to set in and with it the time to take leave. It was the good-bye that I will never forget. Extending her hands, Delena took my hands in hers. Elam and the children surrounded me.

Delena began.

"We have somethin' to say before you leave. Hain't never, I mean never, has anyone done come to our home to eat with us. Not that we hain't invited them. But you came. And you came on Thanksgiving."

Then she paused, her eyes glistening with gratitude and penetrating mine.

"No," she continued, "it wasn't you. Today Jesus himself done come to our home, and we give thanks for the blessing of his presence. We don't have to go anywhere else to look for him 'cuz he is right here, before our eyes, inside our home. We look upon him."

I could say nothing. Delena and Elam, the poorest of the poor, the outcasts, had welcomed me as Jesus, had seen Jesus at their table and in their home. They knew that they were not born 2,000 years too late. They needed neither angel choirs nor a star in the East to proclaim his presence. Like an awkward drummer boy playing his instrument, they worshiped Jesus with the best they had, having found him in a church lady far from home on a holiday.

Exuberance is beauty.
—WILLIAM BLAKE

MINING OUR FAITH, ENRICHING OUR LIFE

When have I humbly realized that someone saw Christ in me?
How did this open my eyes to the beauty of sharing
and to the witness of love?

Songbirds

There's a Chinese proverb, "Keep a green tree in your heart and tend it gently so that birds will come warble in its branches."

What are the songbirds that nestle in the tree of your life? Do they show you how to rest in the niches of ordinary life's branches? Do they sing to you: *Go out on a limb for peace?* Maybe they urge you to glide through each day, one wing beat at a time.

Waiting in line at the grocery store or stopping at a red light provide blessed moments to listen to God in the warbles of our songbirds. Do we hear their symphonies calling us to harmony with creation, their choruses of justice and compassion, their chants of wisdom and wonder?

When I Grow Up

It was the annual "What do you want to be when you grow up?" segment of the first-grade curriculum.

The boys I taught veered toward police officers, firefighters, and one livery driver. My girls saw themselves as mothers, nuns, teachers, and even a dancing nurse.

Molly, a reflective and reticent child, was keeping a low profile. Toward the end of the week, she simply stated: "I know exactly what I want to do when I grow up. I want to help everybody who's anybody or nobody."

There is nothing nobler than turning an act of giving into the art of living.

*Cheerfulness removes the rust from the mind,
lubricates our inward machinery, and
enables us to do our work with fewer creaks
and groans. If people were universally
cheerful, there wouldn't be half the quarreling
or a tenth part of the wickedness there is.
Cheerfulness, too, promotes health and morality.
Cheerful people live longest here on earth,
afterward in our hearts.*

—AUTHOR UNKNOWN

One kind word can warm three winter months.

—JAPANESE PROVERB

An Old-Fashioned Thanksgiving
A Short Story

LOUISA MAY ALCOTT

Sixty years ago, up among the New Hampshire hills, lived Farmer Bassett, with a houseful of sturdy sons and daughters growing up about him. They were poor in money, but rich in land and love, for the wide acres of wood, corn, and pasture land fed, warmed, and clothed the flock, while mutual patience, affection, and courage made the old farmhouse a very happy home.

November had come; the crops were in, and barn, buttery, and bin were overflowing with the harvest that rewarded the summer's hard work. The big kitchen was a jolly place just now, for in the great fireplace roared a cheerful fire; on the walls hung garlands of dried apples, onions, and corn; up aloft from the beams shone crook-necked squashes, juicy hams, and dried venison—for in those days deer still haunted the deep forests, and hunters flourished. Savory smells were in the air; on the crane hung steaming kettles, and down among the red embers copper saucepans simmered, all suggestive of some approaching feast.

A white-headed baby lay in the old blue cradle that had rocked six other babies, now and then lifting his head to look out, like a round, full moon, then subsided to kick and crow contentedly, and suck the rosy apple he had no teeth to bite. Two small boys sat on the wooden settle shelling corn for popping, and picking out the biggest nuts from the goodly store their own hands had gathered in October. Four young girls stood at the long dresser, busily chopping meat, pounding spice, and slicing apples; and the tongues of Tilly, Prue, Roxy, and Rhody went as fast as their hands. Farmer Bassett, and Eph, the oldest boy, were "chorin' 'round" outside, for Thanksgiving was at hand, and all must be in order for that time-honored day.

To and fro, from table to hearth, bustled buxom Mrs. Bassett, flushed and floury, but busy and blithe as the queen bee of this busy little hive should be.

"I do like to begin seasonable and have things to my mind. Thanksgivin' dinners can't be drove, and it does take a sight of victuals to fill all these hungry stomicks," said the good woman, as she gave a vigorous stir to the great kettle of cider applesauce, and cast a glance of housewifely pride at the fine array of pies set forth on the buttery shelves.

"Only one more day and then it will be the time to eat. I didn't take but one bowl of hasty pudding this morning, so I shall have plenty of room when the nice things come," confided Seth to Sol, as he cracked a large hazelnut as easily as a squirrel.

"No need of my starvin' beforehand. I always have room enough, and I'd like to have Thanksgiving every day," answered Solomon, gloating like a young ogre over the little pig that lay near by, ready for roasting.

"Sakes alive, I don't, boys! It's a marcy it don't come but once a year. I should be worn to a thread paper with all this extra work atop of my winter weavin' and spinnin'," laughed their mother, as she plunged her plump arms into the long bread trough and began to knead the dough as if a famine were at hand.

Tilly, the oldest girl, a red-cheeked, black-eyed lass of fourteen, was grinding briskly at the mortar, for spices were costly, and not a grain must be wasted. Prue kept time with the chopper, and the twins sliced away at the apples till their little brown arms ached, for all knew how to work, and did so now with a will.

"I think it's real fun to have Thanksgiving at home. I'm sorry Gran'ma is sick, so we can't go there as usual, but I like to mess 'round here, don't you, girls?" asked Tilly, pausing to take a sniff at the spicy pestle.

"It will be kind of lonesome with only our own folks." "I like to see all the cousins and aunts, and have games, and sing," cried the twins, who were regular little romps, and could run, swim, coast, and shout as well as their brothers.

"I don't care a mite for all that. It will be so nice to eat dinner together, warm and comfortable at home," said quiet Prue, who loved her own cozy nooks like a cat.

"Come, girls, fly 'round and get your chores done, so we can clear away for dinner jest as soon as I clap my bread into the oven," called Mrs. Bassett presently, as she rounded off the last loaf of brown bread which was to feed the hungry mouths that seldom tasted any other.

"Here's a man comin' up the hill lively!" "Guess it's Gad Hopkins. Pa told him to bring a dezzen oranges, if they warn't too high!" shouted Sol and Seth, running to the door, while the girls smacked their lips at the thought of this rare treat, and Baby threw his apple overboard, as if getting ready for a new cargo.

But all were doomed to disappointment, for it was not Gad, with the much-desired fruit. It was a stranger, who threw himself off his horse and hurried up to Mr. Bassett in the yard, with some brief message that made the farmer drop his ax and look so sober that his wife guessed at once some bad news had come; and crying, "Mother's wuss! I know she is!" Out ran the good woman, forgetful of the flour on her arms and the oven waiting for its most important batch.

The man said old Mr. Chadwick, down to Keene, stopped him as he passed, and told him to tell Mrs. Bassett her mother was failin' fast, and she'd better come today. He knew no more, and having delivered his errand he rode away, saying it looked like snow and he must be jogging, or he wouldn't get home till night.

"We must go right off, Eldad. Hitch up, and I'll be ready in less'n no time," said Mrs. Bassett, wasting not a minute in tears and lamentations, but pulling off her apron as she went in, with her head in a sad jumble of bread, anxiety, turkey, sorrow, haste, and cider applesauce.

A few words told the story, and the children left their work to help her get ready, mingling their grief for "Gran'ma" with regrets for the lost dinner.

"I'm dreadful sorry, dears, but it can't be helped. I couldn't cook nor eat no way now, and if that blessed woman gets better sudden, as she has before, we'll have cause for thanksgivin', and I'll give you a dinner you won't forget in a hurry," said Mrs. Bassett, as she tied on her brown silk pumpkin-hood, with a sob for the good old mother who had made it for her.

Not a child complained after that, but ran about helpfully, bringing moccasins, heating the footstone, and getting ready for a long drive, because Gran'ma lived twenty miles away, and there were no railroads in those parts to whisk people to and fro like magic. By the time the old yellow sleigh was at the door, the bread was in the oven, and Mrs. Bassett was waiting, with her camlet cloak on, and the baby done up like a small bale of blankets.

"Now, Eph, you must look after the cattle like a man and keep up the fires, for there's a storm brewin', and neither the children nor dumb critters must suffer," said Mr. Bassett, as he turned up the collar of his rough coat and put on his blue mittens, while the old mare shook her bells as if she preferred a trip to Keene to hauling wood all day.

"Tilly, put extra comfortables on the beds to-night, the wind is so searchin' up chamber. Have the baked beans and Injun-puddin' for dinner, and whatever you do, don't let the boys get at the mince-pies, or you'll have them down sick. I shall come back the minute I can leave Mother. Pa will come to-morrer anyway, so keep snug and be good. I depend on you, my darter; use your jedgment, and don't let nothin' happen while Mother's away."

46

"Yes'm, yes'm—good-bye, good-bye!" called the children, as Mrs. Bassett was packed into the sleigh and driven away, leaving a stream of directions behind her.

Eph, the sixteen-year-old boy, immediately put on his biggest boots, assumed a sober, responsible manner, and surveyed his little responsibilities with a paternal air, drolly like his father's. Tilly tied on her mother's bunch of keys, rolled up the sleeves of her homespun gown, and began to order about the younger girls. They soon forgot poor Granny, and found it great fun to keep house all alone, for Mother seldom left home, but ruled her family in the good old-fashioned way. There were no servants, for the little daughters were Mrs. Bassett's only maids, and the stout boys helped their father, all working happily together with no wages but love; learning in the best manner the use of the heads and hands with which they were to make their own way in the world.

The few flakes that caused the farmer to predict bad weather soon increased to a regular snowstorm, with gusts of wind, for up among the hills winter came early and lingered long. But the children were busy, gay, and warm indoors, and never minded the rising gale nor the whirling white storm outside.

Tilly got them a good dinner, and when it was over the two elder girls went to their spinning, for in the kitchen

47

stood the big and little wheels, and baskets of wool rolls ready to be twisted into yarn for the winter's knitting, and each day brought its stint of work to the daughters, who hoped to be as thrifty as their mother.

Eph kept up a glorious fire, and superintended the small boys, who popped corn and whittled boats on the hearth; while Roxy and Rhody dressed corncob dolls in the settle corner, and Bose, the brindled mastiff, lay on the braided mat, luxuriously warming his old legs. Thus employed, they made a pretty picture, these rosy boys and girls, in their homespun suits, with the rustic toys or tasks which most children nowadays would find very poor or tiresome.

Tilly and Prue sang, as they stepped to and fro, drawing out the smoothly twisted threads to the musical hum of the great spinning wheels. The little girls chattered like magpies over their dolls and the new bedspread they were planning to make, all white dimity stars on a blue calico ground, as a Christmas present to Ma. The boys roared at Eph's jokes, and had rough and tumble games over Bose, who didn't mind them in the least; and so the afternoon wore pleasantly away.

At sunset the boys went out to feed the cattle, bring in heaps of wood, and lock up for the night, as the lonely farmhouse seldom had visitors after dark. The girls got the simple supper of brown bread and milk, baked apples, and a doughnut all 'round as a treat. Then they sat before the fire, the sisters knitting, the brothers with books or games, for Eph loved reading, and Sol and Seth never failed to play a few games of Morris with barley corns, on the little board they had themselves at one corner of the dresser.

"Read out a piece," said Tilly from Mother's chair, where she sat in state, finishing off the sixth woolen sock she had knit that month.

"It's the old history book, but here's a bit you may like, since it's about our folks," answered Eph, turning the yellow page to look at a picture of two quaintly dressed children in some ancient castle.

"Yes, read that. I always like to hear about the Lady Matildy I was named for, and Lord Bassett, Pa's great-great-great-grandpa. He's only a farmer now, but it's nice to know we were somebody two or three hundred years ago," said Tilly, bridling and tossing her curly head as she fancied the Lady Matilda might have done.

"Don't read the queer words, 'cause we don't understand 'em. Tell it," commanded Roxy, from the cradle, where she was drowsily cuddled with Rhody.

"Well, a long time ago, when Charles the First was in prison, Lord Bassett was a true friend to him," began Eph, plunging into his story without delay. "The lord had some

49

papers that would have hung a lot of people if the king's enemies got hold of 'em, so when he heard one day, all of a sudden, that soldiers were at the castle gate to carry him off, he had just time to call his girl to him and say: 'I may be going to my death, but I won't betray my master. There is no time to burn the papers, and I can not take them with me; they are hidden in the old leathern chair where I sit. No one knows this but you, and you must guard them till I come or send you a safe messenger to take them away. Promise me to be brave and silent, and I can go without fear.' You see, he wasn't afraid to die, but he was to seem a traitor. Lady Matildy promised solemnly, and the words were hardly out of her mouth when the men came in, and her father was carried away a prisoner and sent off to the Tower."

"But she didn't cry; she just called her brother, and sat down in that chair, with her head leaning back on those papers, like a queen, and waited while the soldiers hunted the house over for 'em: wasn't that a smart girl?" cried Tilly, beaming with pride, for she was named for this ancestress, and knew the story by heart.

"I reckon she was scared, though, when the men came swearin' in and asked her if she knew anything about it. The boy did his part then, for *he* didn't know, and fired up and stood before his sister; and he says, says he, as bold

50

as a lion: 'If my lord had told us where the papers be, we would die before we would betray him. But we are children and know nothing, and it is cowardly of you to try to fight us with oaths and drawn swords!'"

As Eph quoted from the book, Seth planted himself before Tilly, with the long poker in his hand, saying, as he flourished it valiantly:

"Why didn't the boy take his father's sword and lay about him? I would, if any one was ha'sh to Tilly."

"You bantam! He was only a bit of a boy, and couldn't do anything. Sit down and hear the rest of it," commanded Tilly, with a pat on the yellow head, and a private resolve that Seth should have the largest piece of pie at dinner next day, as reward for his chivalry.

"Well, the men went off after turning the castle out of window, but they said they should come again; so faithful Matildy was full of trouble, and hardly dared to leave the room where the chair stood. All day she sat there, and at night her sleep was so full of fear about it, that she often got up and went to see that all was safe. The servants thought the fright had hurt her wits, and let her be, but Rupert, the boy, stood by her and never was afraid of her queer ways. She was 'a pious maid,' the book says, and often spent the long evenings reading the Bible, with her brother by her, all alone in the great room, with no one to

51

help her bear her secret, and no good news of her father. At last, word came that the king was dead and his friends banished out of England. Then the poor children were in a sad plight, for they had no mother, and the servants all ran away, leaving only one faithful old man to help them."

"But the father did come?" cried Roxy, eagerly.

"You'll see," continued Eph, half telling, half reading. "Matilda was sure he would, so she sat on in the big chair, guarding the papers, and no one could get her away, till one day a man came with her father's ring and told her to give up the secret. She knew the ring, but would not tell until she had asked many questions, so as to be very sure, and while the man answered all about her father and the king, she looked at him sharply. Then she stood up and said, in a tremble, for there was something strange about the man: 'Sir, I doubt you in spite of the ring, and I will not answer till you pull off the false beard you wear, that I may see your face and know if you are my father's friend or foe.' Off came the disguise, and Matilda found it was my lord himself, come to take them with him out of England. He was very proud of that faithful girl, I guess, for the old chair still stands in the castle, and the name keeps in the family, Pa says, even over here, where some of the Bassetts came along with the Pilgrims."

"Our Tilly would have been as brave, I know, and she looks like the old picter down to Gran'ma's, don't she, Eph?" cried Prue, who admired her bold, bright sister very much.

"Well, I think you'd do the settin' part best, Prue, you are so patient. Till would fight like a wild cat, but she can't hold her tongue worth a cent," answered Eph; whereat Tilly pulled his hair, and the story ended with a general frolic.

When the moon-faced clock behind the door struck nine, Tilly tucked up the children under the "extry cornfortables," and having kissed them all around, as Mother did, crept into her own nest, never minding the little drifts of snow that sifted in upon her coverlet between the shingles of the roof, nor the storm that raged without.

As if he felt the need of unusual vigilance, old Bose lay down on the mat before the door, and pussy had the warm hearth all to herself. If any late wanderer had looked in at midnight, he would have seen the fire blazing up again, and in the cheerful glow the old cat blinking her yellow eyes, as she sat bolt upright beside the spinning wheel, like some sort of household goblin, guarding the children while they slept.

When they woke, like early birds, it still snowed, but up the little Bassetts jumped, broke the ice in their jugs, and went down with cheeks glowing like winter apples, after a brisk scrub and scramble into their clothes. Eph was off to the barn, and Tilly soon had a great kettle of mush ready, which, with milk warm from the cows, made a wholesome breakfast for the seven hearty children.

"Now about dinner," said the young housekeeper, as the pewter spoons stopped clattering, and the earthen bowls stood empty.

"Ma said, have what we liked, but she didn't expect us to have a real Thanksgiving dinner, because she won't be here to cook it, and we don't know how," began Prue, doubtfully.

"I can roast a turkey and make a pudding as well as anybody, I guess. The pies are all ready, and if we can't boil vegetables and so on, we don't deserve any dinner," cried Tilly, burning to distinguish herself, and bound to enjoy to the utmost her brief authority.

"Yes, yes!" cried all the boys, "let's have a dinner anyway; Ma won't care, and the good victuals will spoil if they ain't eaten right up."

"Pa is coming tonight, so we won't have dinner till late; that will be real genteel and give us plenty of time," added Tilly, suddenly realizing the novelty of the task she had undertaken.

"Did you ever roast a turkey?" asked Roxy, with an air of deep interest.

"Should you darst to try?" said Rhody, in an awe-stricken tone.

"You will see what I can do. Ma said I was to use my judgment about things, and I'm going to. All you children have got to do is to keep out of the way, and let Prue and me work. Eph, I wish you'd put a fire in the best room, so the little ones can play in there. We shall want the settin' room for the table, and I won't have them pickin' 'round when we get things fixed," commanded Tilly, bound to make her short reign a brilliant one.

"I don't know about that. Ma didn't tell us to," began cautious Eph, who felt that this invasion of the sacred best parlor was a daring step.

"Don't we always do it Sundays and Thanksgivings? Wouldn't Ma wish the children kept safe and warm any-how? Can I get up a nice dinner with four rascals under my feet all the time? Come, now, if you want roast turkey and onions, plum-puddin' and mince-pie, you'll have to do as I tell you, and be lively about it."

Tilly spoke with such spirit, and her suggestion was so irresistible, that Eph gave in, and, laughing good-naturedly, tramped away to heat up the best room, devoutly hoping that nothing serious would happen to punish such audacity.

The young folks delightedly trooped away to destroy the order of that prim apartment with housekeeping under the black horsehair sofa, "horseback-riders" on the arms of the best rocking chair, and an Indian war dance all over the well-waxed furniture. Eph, finding the society of peaceful sheep and cows more to his mind than that of two excited sisters, lingered over his chores in the barn as long as possible, and left the girls in peace.

Now Tilly and Prue were in their glory, and as soon as the breakfast things were out of the way, they prepared for a grand cooking time. They were handy girls, though they had never heard of a cooking school, never touched a piano, and knew nothing of embroidery beyond the samplers which hung framed in the parlor; one ornamented with a pink mourner under a blue weeping willow, the other with this pleasing verse, each word being done in a different color, which gave the effect of a distracted rainbow:

> This sampler neat was worked by me,
> In my twelfth year, Prudence B.

Both rolled up their sleeves, put on their largest aprons, and got out all the spoons, dishes, pots, and pans they could find, "so as to have everything handy," as Prue said.

"Now, sister, we'll have dinner at five; Pa will be here by that time, if he is coming tonight, and be so surprised to find us all ready, for he won't have had any very nice victuals if Gran'ma is so sick," said Tilly, importantly. "I shall give the children a piece at noon" (Tilly meant luncheon); "doughnuts and cheese, with apple pie and cider, will please 'em. There's beans for Eph; he likes cold pork, so we won't stop to warm it up, for there's lots to do, and I don't mind saying to you I'm dreadful dubersome about the turkey."

"It's all ready but the stuffing, and roasting is as easy as can be. I can baste first-rate. Ma always likes to have me, I'm so patient and stiddy, she says," answered Prue, for the responsibility of this great undertaking did not rest upon her, so she took a cheerful view of things.

"I know, but it's the stuffin' that troubles me," said Tilly, rubbing her round elbows as she eyed the immense fowl laid out on a platter before her. "I don't know how much I want, nor what sort of yarbs to put in, and he's so awful big, I'm kind of afraid of him."

"I ain't! I fed him all summer, and he never gobbled at me. I feel real mean to be thinking of gobbling him, poor old chap," laughed Prue, patting her departed pet with an air of mingled affection and appetite.

"Well, I'll get the puddin' off my mind fust, for it ought to bile all day. Put the big kettle on, and see that the spit is clean, while I get ready."

Prue obediently tugged away at the crane, with its black hooks, from which hung the iron teakettle and three-legged pot; then she settled the long spit in the grooves made for it in the tall andirons, and put the dripping pan underneath, for in those days meat was roasted as it should be, not baked in ovens.

Meantime Tilly attacked the plum pudding. She felt pretty sure of coming out right, here, for she had seen her mother do it so many times, it looked very easy. So in went suet and fruit; all sorts of spice, to be sure she got the right ones, and brandy instead of wine. But she forgot both sugar and salt, and tied it in the cloth so tightly that it had no room to swell, so it would come out as heavy as lead and as hard as a cannonball, if the bag did not burst and spoil it all. Happily unconscious of these mistakes, Tilly popped it into the pot, and proudly watched it bobbing about before she put the cover on and left it to its fate.

"I can't remember what flavorin' Ma puts in," she said, when she had got her bread well soaked for stuffing. "Sage and onions and applesauce go with goose, but I can't feel sure of anything but pepper and salt for a turkey."

"Ma puts in some kind of mint, I know, but I forget whether it is spearmint, peppermint, or pennyroyal," answered Prue, in a tone of doubt, but trying to show her knowledge of "yarbs," or, at least, of their names.

"Seems to me it's sweet majoram or summer savory. I guess we'll put both in, and then we are sure to be right. The best is up garret; you run and get some, while I mash the bread," commanded Tilly, diving into the mess.

Away trotted Prue, but in her haste she got catnip and wormwood, for the garret was darkish, and Prue's little nose was so full of the smell of the onions she had been peeling, that everything smelt of them. Eager to be of use, she pounded up the herbs and scattered the mixture with a liberal hand into the bowl.

"It doesn't smell just right, but I suppose it will when it is cooked," said Tilly, as she filled the empty stomach, that seemed aching for food, and sewed it up with the blue yarn, which happened to be handy. She forgot to tie down his legs and wings, but she set him by till his hour came, well satisfied with her work.

"Shall we roast the little pig, too? I think he'd look nice with a necklace of sausages, as Ma fixed him at Christmas," asked Prue, elated with their success.

"I couldn't do it. I loved that little pig, and cried when he was killed. I should feel as if I was roasting the baby," answered Tilly, glancing toward the buttery where piggy hung, looking so pink and pretty it certainly did seem cruel to eat him.

It took a long time to get all the vegetables ready, for, as the cellar was full, the girls thought they would have every sort. Eph helped, and by noon all was ready for cooking, and the cranberry sauce, a good deal scorched, was cooling in the lean-to.

Luncheon was a lively meal, and doughnuts and cheese vanished in such quantities that Tilly feared no one would have an appetite for her sumptuous dinner. The boys assured her they would be starving by five o'clock, and Sol mourned bitterly over the little pig that was not to be served up.

"Now you all go and coast, while Prue and I set the table and get out the best chiny," said Tilly, bent on having her dinner look well, no matter what its other failings might be.

Out came the rough sleds, on went the round hoods, old hats, red cloaks, and moccasins, and away trudged the four younger Bassetts, to disport themselves in the snow, and try the ice down by the old mill, where the great wheel turned and splashed so merrily in the summertime.

Eph took his fiddle and scraped away to his heart's content in the parlor, while the girls, after a short rest, set the table and made all ready to dish up the dinner when that exciting moment came. It was not at all the sort of table we see now, but would look very plain and countrified to us, with its green-handled knives and two-pronged steel forks, its red-and-white china, and pewter platters, scoured till they shone, with mugs and spoons to match, and a brown jug for the cider. The cloth was coarse, but white as snow, and the little maids had seen the blue-eyed flax grow, out of which their mother wove the linen; they had watched and watched while it bleached in the green meadow. They had no napkins and little silver; but the best tankard and Ma's few wedding spoons were set forth in state. Nuts and apples at the corners gave an air, and the place of honor was left in the middle for the oranges yet to come.

"Don't it look beautiful?" said Prue, when they paused to admire the general effect.

"Pretty nice, I think. I wish Ma could see how well we can do it," began Tilly, when a loud howling startled both girls, and sent them flying to the window. The short afternoon had passed so quickly that twilight had come before they knew it, and now, as they looked out through the gathering dusk, they saw four small black figures tearing up the road, to come bursting in, all screaming at once: "The bear, the bear! Eph, get the gun! He's coming, he's coming!"

Eph had dropped his fiddle, and got down his gun before the girls could calm the children enough to tell their story, which they did in a somewhat incoherent manner. "Down in the holler, coastin', we heard a growl," began Sol, with his eyes as big as saucers. "I see him fust lookin' over the wall," roared Seth, eager to get his share of honor.

"Awful big and shaggy," quavered Roxy, clinging to Tilly, while Rhody hid in Prue's skirts, and piped out:

"His great paws kept clawing at us, and I was so scared my legs would hardly go."

"We ran away as fast as we could go, and he came growlin' after us. He's awful hungry, and he'll eat every one of us if he gets in," continued Sol, looking about him for a safe retreat.

"Oh, Eph, don't let him eat us," cried both little girls, flying upstairs to hide under their mother's bed, as their surest shelter.

"No danger of that, you little geese. I'll shoot him as soon as he comes. Get out of the way, boys," and Eph raised the window to get good aim.

"There he is! Fire away, and don't miss!" cried Seth, hastily following Sol, who had climbed to the top of the dresser as a good perch from which to view the approaching fray.

Prue retired to the hearth as if bent on dying at her post rather than desert the turkey, now "browning beautiful," as she expressed it. But Tilly boldly stood at the open window, ready to lend a hand if the enemy proved too much for Eph.

All had seen bears, but none had ever come so near before, and even brave Eph felt that the big brown beast slowly trotting up the dooryard was an unusually formidable specimen. He was growling horribly, and stopped now and then as if to rest and shake himself.

"Get the ax, Tilly, and if I should miss, stand ready to keep him off while I load again," said Eph, anxious to kill his first bear in style and alone; a girl's help didn't count.

Tilly flew for the ax, and was at her brother's side by the time the bear was near enough to be dangerous. He stood on his hind legs, and seemed to sniff with relish the savory odors that poured out of the window.

"Fire, Eph!" cried Tilly, firmly.

"Wait till he rears again. I'll get a better shot then" answered the boy, while Prue covered her ears to shut out the bang, and the small boys cheered from their dusty refuge among the pumpkins.

But a very singular thing happened next, and all who saw it stood amazed, for suddenly Tilly threw down the ax, flung open the door, and ran straight into the arms of the bear, who stood erect to receive her, while his growlings changed to a loud "Haw, haw!" that startled the children more than the report of a gun.

"It's Gad Hopkins, tryin' to fool us!" cried Eph, much disgusted at the loss of his prey, for these hardy boys loved to hunt and prided themselves on the number of wild animals and birds they could shoot in a year.

"Oh, Gad, how could you scare us so?" laughed Tilly, still held fast in one shaggy arm of the bear, while the other drew a dozen oranges from some deep pocket in the buffalo-skin coat, and fired them into the kitchen with such good aim that Eph ducked, Prue screamed, and Sol and Seth came down much quicker than they went up.

"Wal, you see I got upsot over yonder, and the old horse went home while I was floundering in a drift, so I tied on the buffalers to tote 'em easy, and come along till I see the children playin' in the holler. I jest meant to give 'em a little scare, but they run like partridges, and I kep' up the joke to see how Eph would like this sort of company," and Gad haw-hawed again.

"You'd have had a warm welcome if we hadn't found you out. I'd have put a bullet through you in a jiffy, old chap," said Eph, coming out to shake hands with the young giant, who was only a year or two older than himself.

"Come in and set up to dinner with us. Prue and I have done it all ourselves, and Pa will be along soon, I reckon," cried Tilly, trying to escape.

"Couldn't, no ways. My folks will think I'm dead ef I don't get along home, sence the horse and sleigh have gone ahead empty. I've done my arrant and had my joke; now I want my pay, Tilly," and Gad took a hearty kiss from the rosy cheeks of his "little sweetheart," as he called her. His own cheeks tingled with the smart slap she gave him as she ran away, calling out that she hated bears and would bring her ax next time.

"I ain't afeared—your sharp eyes found me out: and ef you run into a bear's arms you must expect a hug," answered Gad, as he pushed back the robe and settled his fur cap more becomingly.

"I should have known you in a minute if I hadn't been asleep when the girls squalled. You did it well, though, and I advise you not to try it again in a hurry, or you'll get shot," said Eph, as they parted, he rather crestfallen and Gad in high glee.

"My sakes alive—the turkey is all burnt one side, and the kettles have biled over so the pies I put to warm are all ashes!" scolded Tilly, as the flurry subsided and she remembered her dinner.

"Well, I can't help it. I couldn't think of victuals when I expected to be eaten alive myself, could I?" pleaded poor Prue, who had tumbled into the cradle when the rain of oranges began.

Tilly laughed, and all the rest joined in, so good humor was restored, and the spirits of the younger ones were revived by sucks from the one orange which passed from hand to hand with great rapidity while the older girls dished up the dinner. They were just struggling to get the pudding out of the cloth when Roxy called out: "Here's Pa!"

"There's folks with him," added Rhody.

"Lots of 'em! I see two big sleighs chock full," shouted Seth, peering through the dusk.

"It looks like a semintary. Guess Gran'ma's dead and come up to be buried here," said Sol, in a solemn tone. This startling suggestion made Tilly, Prue, and Eph hasten to look out, full of dismay at such an ending of their festival.

"If that is a funeral, the mourners are uncommonly jolly," said Eph, dryly, as merry voices and loud laughter broke the white silence without.

"I see Aunt Cinthy, and Cousin Hetty—and there's Mose and Amos. I do declare, Pa's bringin' 'em all home to have some fun here," cried Prue, as she recognized one familiar face after another.

"Oh, my patience! Ain't I glad I got dinner, and don't I hope it will turn out good!" exclaimed Tilly, while the twins pranced with delight, and the small boys roared:

"Hooray for Pa! Hooray for Thanksgivin'!"

The cheer was answered heartily, and in came Father, Mother, Baby, aunts, and cousins, all in great spirits; and all much surprised to find such a festive welcome awaiting them.

"Ain't Gran'ma dead at all?" asked Sol, in the midst of the kissing and handshaking.

"Bless your heart, no! It was all a mistake of old Mr. Chadwick's. He's as deaf as an adder, and when Mrs. Brooks told him Mother was mendin' fast, and she wanted me to come down today, certain sure, he got the message all wrong, and give it to the fust person passin' in such a way as to scare me 'most to death, and send us down in a hurry. Mother was sittin' up as chirk as you please, and dreadful sorry you didn't all come."

"So, to keep the house quiet for her, and give you a taste of the fun, your Pa fetched us all up to spend the evenin', and we are goin' to have a jolly time on't, to jedge by the looks of things," said Aunt Cinthy, briskly finishing the tale when Mrs. Bassett paused for want of breath.

"What in the world put it into your head we was comin', and set you to gittin' up such a supper?" asked Mr. Bassett, looking about him, well pleased and much surprised at the plentiful table.

Tilly modestly began to tell, but the others broke in and sang her praises in a sort of chorus, in which bears, pigs, pies, and oranges were oddly mixed. Great satisfaction was expressed by all, and Tilly and Prue were so elated by the commendation of Ma and the aunts, that they set forth their dinner, sure everything was perfect.

But when the eating began, which it did the moment wraps were off, then their pride got a fall; for the first person who tasted the stuffing (it was big Cousin Mose, and that made it harder to bear) nearly choked over the bitter morsel.

"Tilly Bassett, whatever made you put wormwood and catnip in your stuffin'?" demanded Ma, trying not to be severe, for all the rest were laughing, and Tilly looked ready to cry.

"I did it," said Prue, nobly taking all the blame, which caused Pa to kiss her on the spot, and declare that it didn't do a mite of harm, for the turkey was all right.

"I never see onions cooked better. All the vegetables is well done, and the dinner a credit to you, my dears," declared Aunt Cinthy, with her mouth full of the fragrant vegetable she praised.

The pudding was an utter failure in spite of the blazing brandy in which it lay—as hard and heavy as one of the stone balls on Squire Dunkin's great gate. It was speedily whisked out of sight, and all fell upon the pies, which were perfect. But Tilly and Prue were much depressed, and didn't recover their spirits till dinner was over and the evening fun well under way.

"Blind-man's bluff," "Hunt the slipper," "Come, Philander," and other lively games soon set everyone bubbling over with jollity, and when Eph struck up "Money Musk" on his fiddle, old and young fell into their places for a dance. All down the long kitchen they stood, Mr. and Mrs. Bassett at the top, the twins at the bottom, and then away they went, heeling and toeing, cutting pigeon-wings, and taking their steps in a way that would convulse modern children with their new-fangled romps called dancing. Mose and Tilly covered themselves with glory by the vigor with which they kept it up, till fat Aunt Cinthy fell into a chair, breathlessly declaring that a very little of such exercise was enough for a woman of her "heft."

Apples and cider, chat and singing, finished the evening, and after a grand kissing all round, the guests drove away in the clear moonlight which came out to cheer their long drive.

When the jingle of the last bell had died away, Mr. Bassett said soberly, as they stood together on the hearth:

"Children, we have special cause to be thankful that the sorrow we expected was changed into joy, so we'll read a chapter 'fore we go to bed, and give thanks where thanks is due."

Then Tilly set out the light stand with the big Bible on it, and a candle on each side, and all sat quietly in the firelight, smiling as they listened with happy hearts to the sweet old words that fit all times and seasons so beautifully.

When the good-nights were over, and the children in bed, Prue put her arm round Tilly and whispered tenderly, for she felt her shake, and was sure she was crying:

"Don't mind about the old stuffin' and puddin', deary— nobody cared, and Ma said we really did do surprisin' well for such young girls."

The laughter Tilly was trying to smother broke out then, and was so infectious, Prue could not help joining her, even before she knew the cause of the merriment.

"I was mad about the mistakes, but don't care enough to cry. I'm laughing to think how Gad fooled Eph and I found him out. I thought Mose and Amos would have died over it, when I told them, it was so funny," explained Tilly, when she got her breath.

"I was so scared that when the first orange hit me, I thought it was a bullet, and scrabbled into the cradle as fast as I could. It was real mean to frighten the little ones so," laughed Prue, as Tilly gave a growl.

Here a smart rap on the wall of the next room caused a sudden lull in the fun, and Mrs. Bassett's voice was heard, saying warningly, "Girls, go to sleep immediate, or you'll wake the baby."

"Yes'm," answered two meek voices, and after a few irrepressible giggles, silence reigned, broken only by an occasional snore from the boys, or the soft scurry of mice in the buttery, taking their part in this old-fashioned Thanksgiving.

The best is yet to be.
—ROBERT BROWNING

Hymns and Spiritual
Songs of Thanks

For the Beauty of the Earth

FOLLIOTT S. PIERPOINT

For the beauty of the earth,
For the glory of the skies;
For the love which from our birth,
Over and around us lies;

Refrain: Lord of all, to Thee we raise
            This, our hymn of grateful praise.

For the wonder of each hour,
Of the day and of the night;
Hill and vale and tree and flow'r,
Sun and moon, and stars of light;

Refrain

For the joy of ear and eye,
For the heart and mind's delight;
For the mystic harmony,
Linking sense to sound and sight;

Refrain

For the joy of human love,
Brother, sister, parent, child;
Friends on Earth and friends above,
For all gentle thoughts and mild;

Refrain

For Thy church that evermore,
Lifteth holy hands above;
Off'ring up on ev'ry shore,
Her pure sacrifice of love;

Refrain

For the martyrs' crown of light,
For Thy prophets' eagle eye,
For Thy bold confessors' might,
For the lips of infancy;

Refrain

For Thy virgins' robes of snow,
For Thy maiden mother mild,
For Thyself, with hearts aglow,
Jesu, Victim undefiled;

Refrain

For Thyself, best Gift Divine,
To the world so freely given,
For that great, great love of Thine,
Peace on earth and joy in heaven;

Refrain

Thanks to God

AUGUST L. STORM

Thanks to God for my Redeemer,

Thanks for all Thou dost provide!

Thanks for times now but a memory,

Thanks for Jesus by my side!

Thanks for pleasant, balmy springtime,

Thanks for dark and stormy fall!

Thanks for tears by now forgotten,

Thanks for peace within my soul!

Thanks for prayers that Thou hast answered,

Thanks for what Thou dost deny!

Thanks for storms that I have weathered,

Thanks for all Thou dost supply!

Thanks for pain, and thanks for pleasure,

Thanks for comfort in despair!

Thanks for grace that none can measure,

Thanks for love beyond compare!

Thanks for roses by the wayside,

Thanks for thorns their stems contain!

Thanks for home and thanks for fireside,

Thanks for hope, that sweet refrain!

Thanks for joy and thanks for sorrow,

Thanks for heav'nly peace with Thee!

Thanks for hope in the tomorrow,
Thanks through all eternity!

(CF. EPHESIANS 5:20)

Count Your Blessings

JOHNSON OATMAN JR.

When upon life's billows you are tempest tossed,
When you are discouraged, thinking all is lost,
Count your many blessings, name them one by one,
And it will surprise you what the Lord hath done.

Refrain:

> Count your blessings, name them one by one,
> Count your blessings, see what God hath done!
> Count your blessings, name them one by one,
> And it will surprise you what the Lord hath done.

Are you ever burdened with a load of care?
Does the cross seem heavy you are called to bear?
Count your many blessings, every doubt will fly,
And you will keep singing as the days go by.

Refrain

When you look at others with their lands and gold,
Think that Christ has promised you His wealth untold;
Count your many blessings. Wealth can never buy
Your reward in heaven, nor your home on high.

Refrain

So, amid the conflict whether great or small,
Do not be disheartened, God is over all;
Count your many blessings, angels will attend,
Help and comfort give you to your journey's end.

Refrain

(CF. PROVERBS 10:6)

We Gather Together

translated from German to English by
THEODORE BAKER

We gather together to ask the Lord's blessing;
He chastens and hastens His will to make known.
The wicked oppressing now cease from distressing.
Sing praises to His Name; He forgets not His own.

Beside us to guide us, our God with us joining,
Ordaining, maintaining His kingdom divine;
So from the beginning the fight we were winning;
Thou, Lord, were at our side, all glory be Thine!

We all do extol Thee, Thou Leader triumphant,
And pray that Thou still our Defender will be.
Let Thy congregation escape tribulation;
Thy Name be ever praised! O Lord, make us free!

(CF. LUKE 13:10–17)

Come, ye thankful people come

HENRY ALFORD

Come, ye thankful people, come,
Raise the song of harvest home!
All is safely gathered in,
Ere the winter storms begin;
God, our Maker, doth provide
For our wants to be supplied;
Come to God's own temple, come;
Raise the song of harvest home!

We ourselves are God's own field,
Fruit unto his praise to yield;
Wheat and tares together sown
Unto joy or sorrow grown;
First the blade and then the ear,
Then the full corn shall appear;
Grant, O harvest Lord, that we
Wholesome grain and pure may be.

For the Lord our God shall come,
And shall take the harvest home;
From His field shall in that day
All offences purge away,
Giving angels charge at last

In the fire the tares to cast;
But the fruitful ears to store
In the garner evermore.

Then, thou Church triumphant come,
Raise the song of harvest home!
All be safely gathered in,
Free from sorrow, free from sin,
There, forever purified,
In God's garner to abide;
Come, ten thousand angels, come,
Raise the glorious harvest home!

You have turned my mourning into dancing;
you have taken off my sackcloth
and clothed me with joy,
so that my soul may praise you and not be silent.
O LORD my God, I will give thanks to you for ever.

—PSALM 30:11–12

A Psalm of Thanksgiving

Make a joyful noise to the Lord, all the earth.
    Worship the LORD with gladness;
    come into his presence with singing.
Know that the LORD is God.
    It is he that made us, and we are his;
    we are his people, and the sheep of his pasture.
Enter his gates with thanksgiving,
    and his courts with praise.
    Give thanks to him, bless his name.
For the LORD is good;
    his steadfast love endures for ever,
    and his faithfulness to all generations.

—PSALM 100

Closing Prayers

Thou that has given so much to me,
Give one thing more—a grateful heart;
Not thankful when it pleaseth me,
As if thy blessings had spare days;
But such a heart, whose pulse may be
Thy praise.

—GEORGE HERBERT

Bless us, O Lord,
and these thy gifts which
we are about to receive from thy bounty,
through Christ, Our Lord.
Amen.

—ANONYMOUS

And let the peace of Christ rule in your hearts,
to which indeed you were called in the one body.
And be thankful.

—COLOSSIANS 3:15

Almighty and gracious Father,

we give you thanks

for the fruits of the earth in their season

and for the labors of those who harvest them.

Make us, we pray,

faithful stewards of your great bounty,

for the provision of our necessities

and the relief of all who are in need,

to the glory of your Name;

through Jesus Christ our Lord,

who lives and reigns with

you and the Holy Spirit,

one God, now and for ever. Amen.

—BOOK OF COMMON PRAYER

You are the peace of all things calm

You are the place to hide from harm

You are the light that shines in dark

You are the heart's eternal spark

You are the door that's open wide

You are the guest who waits inside

You are the stranger at the door

You are the calling of the poor

You are my Lord and with me still

You are my love, keep me from ill

You are the light, the truth, the way

You are my Savior this very day.

—TRADITIONAL CELTIC PRAYER

Yours, O Lord, are the greatness, the power, the glory, the victory, and the majesty; for all that is in the heavens and on the earth is yours; yours is the kingdom, O Lord, and you are exalted as head above all. Riches and honor come from you, and you rule over all. In your hand are power and might; and it is in your hand to make great and to give strength to all. And now, our God, we give thanks to you and praise your glorious name.

—1 CHRONICLES 29:11–13

Lord, make me an instrument of Your peace;
Where there is hatred, let me sow love.
Where there is injury, pardon.
Where there is doubt, faith.
Where there is despair, hope.
Where there is darkness, light.
Where there is sadness, joy.

—attributed to ST. FRANCIS OF ASSISI

10 Blessings in My Life at This Moment

You might consider making this a new tradition around your Thanksgiving table. Either before or after you partake of your feast, take turns going around the table and answering this simple question: "What are ten blessings in your life right now?" As each person responds, encourage the others to listen carefully and respectfully, and leave any questions for later. Simply allow thanksgivings and gratefulness to fill your home.

(RECORD YOUR THOUGHTS HERE.)

About Paraclete Press

WHO WE ARE

Paraclete Press is a publisher of books, recordings, and DVDs on Christian spirituality. Our publishing represents a full expression of Christian belief and practice—from Catholic to Evangelical, from Protestant to Orthodox.

We are the publishing arm of the Community of Jesus, an ecumenical monastic community in the Benedictine tradition. As such, we are uniquely positioned in the marketplace without connection to a large corporation and with informal relationships to many branches and denominations of faith.

WHAT WE ARE DOING

BOOKS

Paraclete publishes books that show the richness and depth of what it means to be Christian. Although Benedictine spirituality is at the heart of all that we do, we publish books that reflect the Christian experience across many cultures, time periods, and houses of worship. We publish books that nourish the vibrant life of the church and its people—books about spiritual practice, formation, history, ideas, and customs.

We have several different series, including the best-selling Paraclete Essentials and Paraclete Giants series of classic texts in contemporary English; A Voice from the

Monastery—men and women monastics writing about living a spiritual life today; award-winning literary faith fiction and poetry; and the Active Prayer Series that brings creativity and liveliness to any life of prayer.

RECORDINGS

From Gregorian chant to contemporary American choral works, our music recordings celebrate sacred choral music through the centuries. Paraclete distributes the recordings of the internationally acclaimed choir Gloriæ Dei Cantores, praised for their "rapt and fathomless spiritual intensity" by *American Record Guide,* and the Gloriæ Dei Cantores Schola, which specializes in the study and performance of Gregorian chant. Paraclete is also the exclusive North American distributor of the recordings of the Monastic Choir of St. Peter's Abbey in Solesmes, France, long considered to be a leading authority on Gregorian chant.

DVDS

Our DVDs offer spiritual help, healing, and biblical guidance for life issues: grief and loss, marriage, forgiveness, anger management, facing death, and spiritual formation.

Learn more about us at our website:
www.paracletepress.com, or call us toll-free at 1-800-451-5006.

You may also be interested in...

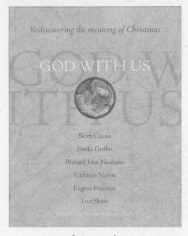

God With Us

Rediscovering the Meaning of Christmas

ISBN: 978-1-55725-541-9 29.95, Hardcover

God With Us is a companion for those who want to experience Christmas as the early Christians once did, set in the larger context of Advent and Epiphany. Through daily meditations, Scripture, prayer, illuminating history, and fine art, we experience what saints have glimpsed through the ages—the wonder of God made flesh.

Contributors: Scott Cairns, Emilie Griffin, Richard John Neuhaus, Kathleen Norris, Eugene Peterson, Luci Shaw

Edited by Greg Pennoyer and Gregory Wolfe

The Christmas Countdown
Creating 25 Days of New Advent Traditions for Families

MARGIE J. HARDING

ISBN: 978-1-55725-698-0 15.99, Paperback

Prepare your heart and home for a meaningful Christmas!

This book provides easy-to-use devotionals with Scripture, music, food, and fun family activities to prepare your heart and home— and reach out to others—in celebration of Christ's coming.

"The Christmas Countdown *reminds us that Christmas is more than a shopping list. This book isn't simply another list of things-to-do this December but rather it is a plea to stop 'doing' and begin 'being' once more. Twenty-five new traditions remind us that family is a gift which reflects the great Gift of God incarnate, restoring us to the beauty of Christmas."*
—Joel Kurz, Pastor, The Garden Community, Baltimore

Available from most booksellers or through Paraclete Press
www.paracletepress.com 1-800-451-5006
Try your local bookstore first.